JOHN BOWIE

KU-246-517

Walking
Towards
The Noise

BRISTOL NOIR

Also by John Bowie

Dead Birds & Sinking Ships

Untethered

Transference

Division

Viking

Weston-super-Nightmare

Curated by John Bowie

Tainted Hearts & Dirty Hell-Hounds

Savage Minds & Raging Bulls

Praise for Bowie's Poetry

'Brutal and lyrical. A wonderful collection.'

— *B F Jones, author of Something Happened at 2 a.m.*

'An Earthshackled-romantic body of work.'

— *Gabriel Hart, author of Virgins In Reverse and The Intrusion; singer/songwriter of Jail Weddings.*

'Evoking Bukowski at times and giving us moving tales of youth alongside paeans and laments.'

— *Scott Cumming, poet, A chapbook About Nothing*

JOHN BOWIE

Walking

Towards

The Noise

~ Poems ~
2020 - 2022

JOHN BOWIE

BRISTOL NOIR

9

JOHN BOWIE

for you

11

contents

MASK ON

MASK OFF

MASK ON

.

a child by time

with ashen skin
and driftwood bones
wrapped in skin, sagging,
like arid wrinkled sheets.
marked, telling of a long, well-weathered life.
but those eyes
say otherwise.

made a child by time;
less hope and strength
as each second drifts, fades.
deemed invisible by the winds
rains and rays
that carry on long after
the last shade of flesh
fades
to a dull ember then
out.

with eyes
growing younger
appreciating their insignificance
until
finally
they'll close, forever.

a heart full of hate

when did the hugs become
shouts?
words softly whispered,
deafening yells.
the tears of joy,
into distilled drops of despair.
did the river dry?
or,
was it always bare?

did the one you love
not love you back?
did (s)he leave?
was birth not connection
enough?
or, was the stone always cold;
impervious to care?

I remember being little, playing in snow
my hands freezing.
the true pain would be, not outside in the cold,
but when you cupped them and
your breaths tried to thaw me,
like your love,
with those stabbing needles.

azure

let's cry,
and
smile together.
as time's tides offer up words
to the shoreline.

as these feet touch sands,
and our minds dance
with crumbling white horses,
that crash fury-filled waves
tempered by magic.

deep blue inks of our
untempered selves.
treasure that shines,
beneath the waves,
defying hardening sands.

love glittering past razor shells,
toughened weeds,
life's wreckage;
cracked stars.

and

as the waters eventually retreat,
the ink slowly fading,
to take us with it.
love endures, captured by rays,

breaking clouds;
casting our words into
—eternity.

back

a sudden torrent, a wash of
panic, anxiety-driven orders for
lock-ins,
isolation.
as regret grows into trees of hurt at not savouring that
last
simple hug we could have had.
and months roll into years
as family faces become harder to restore.
hoping it passes,
so we can see them
before they do too: pass.
and for it to be without a mask,
less distance,
eye to eye
to feel the warmth in a touch.

then, snap—we're back.
like the graves aren't filled
and the years of stolen moments
didn't happen.
as if the person before you
is the same as before,
when, really we're all
a little colder to touch,
left untrusting,
time lost,
left with older, bitter, aged monsters—
that rage inside.

bluebells

Winter falls
as Spring delights—
glistening and sparkling.
last season's dead and dying,
lie crested with a kiss of moss.
as steam rises through
rays of sun-ripened air.

virgin footsteps
break nature's blanket.
as birds' song
caress
and trees dance.

before witnesses
reach a blessed canvas.
a floor littered with
bells, ringing out
—a wash of bluest inks.

songs marry to the trees,
soil and flowers.
as the morning's feud melts
waiting for
nature's opus to cry out for more—
passionate chords,
fresh blossoms of hope.
tempering harsh words that fell,
like coldest winter

that now scatter, fading,
melting into Spring,
with spectrums of blue and purest light.

bouldering

birthed onto shore from ferocious waters,
left to navigate unknown sands,
towards a rocky face.
with
companions that come and go.
some help,
others knock you sideways,
then, some look to push you back down
into the waves below.
whilst the ones that last—do all three.

you get cut on the way up,
battered as you grasp to hold on,
knowing it hurts and slices anyway
to make—progress.
left with scars, by moments
trying to succeed.
advancing invisible marks, with you till the end.

if you fall, that's it—the end.
but, if you do make it, to the top; old, exhausted,
full of cuts, with or without someone to share,
by then it's over and time to return to the sea.
and that climb,
was it worth it?

bristol noir

tainted hearts & dirty hellhounds
fragile paper sheets heavy with
powerful words
savage minds & raging bulls
sensitive creators
wielding unflinching blows.

here be demons
and generous, wordsmiths, gifting us access
to their souls.

noir writers. soldiers and nurses—one and all.
penned strength, resilience, a crutch in each stroke.
allowing escape into lines;
remembered and cherished.

tainted hearts and savage minds,
sharing magic.
in which to learn, love and lose yourself.
as prose shapes and opens doors
to escape from these crazy-mad times.

welcome readers, here be demons.
the best kind,
but, remember...
these are the writers that queue by you,
stand next to you,
walk behind you.
impatient to return to a bloodthirsty keyboard,

to execute with words.

remember,
you can always close the book, return to the true horror
show:
outside—
where those writers prowl, researching the next
killer inside themselves.

concrete and fire

they said:
we're going to see the Dragon Lady,
the Witch,
the Ancient Hag.
a scary old woman.
she's got teeth like razors,
long spindly arms,
with claws at the ends.
she'll chase us,
you'll love it,
you in?
or, are you a little chicken?

I was scared of them.
trembling at that rabble of
wastrel street dogs,
lost lamentable lads.
yet, much more than scared of them, or of this
Dragon Lady they'd conjured.
I was scared of fitting in:

if I did...
and if I didn't.

these street dogs had nothing,
roamed red brick and concrete streets,
fixed in a sprawling prison.
bored.
breaking what little they owned

while stealing other peoples'
to break some more,
with nothing,
they still didn't know what they really wanted.
other than to destroy,

and,

to taunt this poor old lady.
shaped into an image,
to target;
a witch
to pin their frustrations on.
like paining her
would
make the
weeping concrete walls of those council estates turn to
butter
and melt away to a better place.

on the approach to the Dragon Lady's house
I saw it was my own gran's—a great one at that.
and part of me died.
knowing I was married to the mob that would taunt her.

the Dragon breathed hardest
the day after the event.
when I sat on her lap,
as I told her...lied:
no, I wasn't one of them.

her eyes scorched through,
searing my deceit.
those wise eyes...knowing my plight.
fear of not fitting in,
and terrified if I ever did.

knowing I never would.

then came a smile of the ages
and the touch of that wise old hand,
consoling,
dowsing flames of shame
on a young foolish lad's skin.

eventually,

I was sent away from them all,
and her.
I never saw if those estate walls ever melted for the mob.
to reveal a place more magical than the Dragon's lair.
instead, I was hidden from the raging conflict inside of
them all.
as tears built, knowing it would always be there in me.
as it is now.
deep inside.
memories like burning twisted shrapnel,
you can't untouch those flames.
of a young lad's mistake
struggling to fit in.
although,
the old Dragon Lady did try.

cycles of being

what a difference a day makes?
a month.
as cells turn over so efficiently.
is there any single being,
a day to the next?
a constant.
or, is it all flux, morphing,
changing,
a transient evolution
nature's inevitable chorus,
played out on our own bodies—before our eyes.
as the mirror slowly decays,
and the workings of comprehension stall,
grind,
falter.

like a robot with rechargeable batteries,
fixing itself over and over.
remade,
as power cells fade
and the
core diminishes.

emotions, like our skin,
change the only constant:
one day we're up,
the other we're down.
addled by hurt, then—
a joy-filled balloon drifting up to the stars.

dying man's grace

the pipes are in,
bedsores multiply.
with
cuts and bruises to
paper-thin skin.
pride dropped, through
dirty bed sheets
confidence waning in
every emptied bedpan.

a controlling life's
end
delayed
in a room full of others.
sharing it all: sheets,
the care.

far away from that car driven too fast,
parked on the drive
so neighbours could see it,
outside a house you
designed yourself
—soon to be knocked
down.
full of clothes and things
you overthought and
overbought
gathered for show—labels
and cost,

now worthless.

with pride stripped;
true worth laid bare,
you can hold that head
high.
knowing you knew what
you wanted back then,
when you could,
and were confident
enough,
to go hard and
get it.

and now it's gone.
every second day's
memories resurface clear
enough
to remind you:
you made it.
and on those other days...
it's like you were never
there at all—but we
know—remember and we
see:
the pride was then,
the grace is now.

so, be free, forevermore.
on pillows of our own
making, in achievements
in all of us you leave
behind.

—rest in peace

peoples' faces in cars passing by

time's tides in the belly of a kitten,
marred by a melee of torrid thoughts.
as ruptured spines teeter on the wings of warring angels.
we are everywhere and nowhere at all,
every one of us sewn together
by the slightest glance of a smiling child.
and the barbs and razor-sharp steel of reality laid bare;
battling invisible monsters,
failed efforts.
readying to succeed,
whilst built to fail.
and then we finish, only to
start over again the next day
in another life.
destined to forever be smothered
in our beautiful pained reincarnations.

funeral springboard

the fire lit
we parked
as birds watched
the casket was about to roll
a small gathering waited
to enter
to witness the final stop

they didn't see the resting crows
silence in the trees
nature's audience

in the background
of a painted backdrop,
the ancients called
shining ebbs of lives.
on their way in
and out of
time's concerto filled with
blooms
and decay

I started my run at its hues
past
the crematorium,
cars,
people,
a tired father holding programmes
that shouted happy dead memories on the cover

34

I ran at that hill; answered its call
replied to those slopes
didn't stop 'till the summit
my lungs burst
eyes exploded
by
the cresting sights from the top
and those lives, so small at the bottom
—tiny specs moving
in and out of lustre, life and dismay

me,
spent
I could die there
buried with the hillside's song
on its flower-blanketed sides
as I'm forgotten
and in the valley
the funeral crowd finally enters
to mourn
another.

JOHN BOWIE

MASK OFF

37

grasp the nettle

we all remember the pain as a child,
brushing gently
against those little innocuous plants.
always guarding the places we loved to play.
waiting to pounce.
they didn't stop us.
eventually, the tears passed—
the games continued.

older,
we're told to stand up to…
face up to…
—and ride it out.

that we must, grasp it.
and told that what hurts, will make us harder.

what hurts most…is realising,
that the nettles of our past
left seeds, barbs and pins.
and now we carry the harshest sting.
drawing tears from small faces,
looking into innocent eyes of reason
and cupped by little hands that haven't even brushed
their first nettle
—yet.

graveyard of content

at No.17 she creaks low,
Winter biting her hips.
her hold shakes holding a few tins and a milk carton
like lead weights.
her strength stolen by years.
muscle wasted,
a savage city took its toll.
she rides out remaining hours
—hungry, cold, alone.

at No.27 they bounce out a
front door that crashes open
on hinges they can afford to replace.
their recycling overflows:
boxes, wasted food, unneeded tat and
luxury half-touched crap
—food for foxes, scavengers and rats.

at No.32 they diligently separate
plastics and metals too.
they cut down on plastic,
to save the seas and oceans
—ones they'll never see.

back at No.17 she takes her time
as the rest of the street rush, clatter and are gone.
their entire house loads, waste, and a badge of
consumption.
as she slowly creaks in and out.

a ghost. a statue. invisible to touch.
only those few tins,
a plastic milk carton—rationed supply.
not enough to live on.
she can't see where they go, her companions.
these tins and a carton.
now they leave her too.
like the last touch of a friend.
falling to the floor.

milky cataracts attack her senses.
she looks at blurred images:
masses of piled up waste by other houses
—enough to feed her till Spring.

the street works hard to save the oceans
and those fish they'll never see.
their huge TV screens told them to.

at No.17 she's dying,
colder, always alone,
now more than ever.
and hungrier than hell.
on the street that never saw her pass.
no more than the Indian Ocean
and Atlantic's blues.
invisible past the piles of their self-righteous
separation of waste.
divided into those coloured plastic containers.

at No.17 she's dead,
separated from life.
last breaths recorded in stiff sheets, then lost,
as tears of condensation roll,
drip,
then fall

to a dusty carpet. a pitiful embrace.

bin collectors come and go—reapers in the night.
and
they leave No.17's three tin cans
and a milk carton.
they
weren't in the right boxes.

heels in a storm

they didn't see a thing, not for sure
a fur-lined flicker past the window.
a glimpse, but not forgotten
Coleridge's folly
Wordsworth never wore fur
Wilde, maybe...

this was different.
she was a force of nature,
with fur coat and steel knickers
a fur-coated fury
—carried by blood-red stilettos through a storm.

this kitty barked.

that cosy seaside boozer...was about to ignite.
like an angry storm in a teacup.
the door smashed open with the wind in her hands.
faces growing damp, the sea and rain on her hair.

old dogs, fishermen and farmers
moved quick as she parted the waves.
she would have her seat at the bar,
and the lesser men she'd draw into her web
finding their place too,
to rest
on the morning's shore,
under tomorrow's shingle, driftwood and sand.

in vivo

by the end, it's too late,
the damage done.
by the end, the results are in—
the jury's set.

hoping for more,
mistakes made,
hard borders.

with only love left behind,
and dust to follow.

no resitting, no reruns.

moments themselves,
made precious by their passing.
memories to reflect,
plugged into the last minutes of lucidity.

by the end…
it is, only that.

journey

chasing that 'happy'.
missing moments,
days filled by nagging holes,
anxieties.
troubled
unfulfilled wants.
contrived and held in ever-moving horizons
washed, filtered and tempered
in liquid despair.
remade and re-enforced
in every screen touched
and seen.

like a wilting flower looking to
tomorrow's decaying mass of soil
through turbulent winds
never witnessing
that last random blossom
or,
rays through clouds.

day-to-day joys,
lost.
those in a touch,
smile,
the smallest of hands
growing larger each day,
senses, scents.
transient gifts in nature—coming and going,

like the person
and self.

wake up—now
let go.

or, sleep forever on this train
as your head vibrates painfully against that window
passing scenery, beauty
as you chase
an unknown destination, masked with false
hope by design—
to keep you onboard,
focused on the soil, not the growing flower,
till the end.
and by then, you'll be decaying in it,
and all the flowers too.

just for one day

when hurt-filled torrents drove hard,
even you failed to see why I'd swim against them

captive of burning-hurt
absent touches
no one knew but us

but, it was there, behind a child's eyes and in
each laden step as more life opened the void

heavy little soul, God bless, never carried
eventually...validated
respite found in *another* bottle, disposed seductions
over and over—resurfaced being
every man, woman and child deserve to
sail bitter currents. dream. be a hero.

if,

just for one day

winding time and
erasing the pain and the grit of your

controlling smile, perfect teeth hiding
an agony of deceit, a desperation of
neglect and abandonment

burning hurt braved

ended torment, soothed by the embrace of warm
arms—blood pumping rushing
to the heart of my heart just for one day.

tired eyes watching the imaginary movie of
happiness
ending in the
mess of unravelled, mangled, torn tape

forever and ever.

Collaboration with B F Jones

masks and faces

there are people there, but, I don't see them.
just those masks.
the eyes are there, still.
but, are silenced too.
once the windows to a person.
this thing robbed them.
all these eyes—fragile weathered buoys,
bobbing in troubled,
uncertain waters.

before this, they'd look away, or, embrace
contact.
in a different mask. one of self-image—broadcasting,
shining.
now, all these hollow eyes,
stare,
scared, desolate,
unsure.

who's behind the mask?
their own,
and the rest.
what will be left when masks come off?
everyone trapped in a mass game of 'pass the parcel',
bounced around by decisions made out of their control,
as the contents of the prize slowly decays.

the eyes—all that's left:
no longer glow...only faint embers,

in hope—that when those masks *do* come off
there's still the person underneath
to reignite a flame,
to shine again.

möbius strip

you're in,
you're out.
your favour only ever paper-thin,
and less than that in the rain.

banshee cries—
through a recurrent cycle: hurt, pain, pleasure, joy.
seamlessly attuned to the cycles of the moon.
transient pleasures,
relentless nagging hurt.
love
& hate.
blood let,
but, never dying.

and then it starts all over again...

you're in,
you're out.
as your favour, like your sanity, grows paper-thin.
knowing—it'd be even less, if you were left forgotten,
out in that rain,
like the blood and moon,
always comes.

nothing left, still losing

after each refusal, look,
stare and shrug,
still, he goes back.
when the ego has left the shell
only self-pity remains.
still,
back up to them and
asking:
what can he do for them?

but, they know.
it's really what he wants from them.
and what they have is costly
for a man with
nothing left to give.

but the act.

of confidence,
of the shadow puppet performance,
of the man.
drenched in a
pretence of still being in one piece.
like the man before, he started trying again,
only to be ripped apart,
by claws,
teeth,
of refusal
and disinterest.

a battlefield of desire,
only the true survive.

outlook

you can choose to hold life's knife
by the handle
or blade.

walk past those stinging nettles
or
run straight through.

face the music
or be ignorant to
a new tune.

you can choose *I do*
or
forever wonder w*hat if?*

if you choose the blade
you can learn to live with the pain.
to grip it so tightly
you're cut to the bone.
and the prospect of that comfortable handle
seems unquestionably
dull.

pandemic eyes

like a window to a distant war,
but only a city away.
Zoom screen tiredness
they've lead-weighted weary eyes
having seen Death's eager conveyor
first hand.
shifts: every day and every night.
but for this one, the one they choose
to see *you* on-screen instead.

just another silent NHS hero, and friend.
gracefully
giving up their time, transferring
and breathing life—
to extend another's.
fighting those invisible tiny monsters,
hiding in our germs of attrition,
filth, ignorance
and the disease
that follows.

remember

those daff's we picked
bright yellow
a joy
they soon fell apart,
died.
and, those stones from the beach
smooth and perfectly rounded—like mini-eggs, planets,
another world on their surface.
we lost some,
the kids threw the rest in a hedge.

remember that great window,
a giant stone arch framing the bluest waters
it collapsed. but stood long enough for me to ask you to
marry me.
and, Chuck, he died.
long after he wrote the song that was our first dance
at our wedding.

and, can you see it?
that shirt I wore on our honeymoon,
azure, deepest blue.
like the waters we rode after I proposed.
now, it's faded, shrunk and frayed.
then,
there's us.
with memories, trinkets and faltering keepsakes
we're still here:
ageing, creaking and falling apart

with a glorious patina
to our lasting
love.

MASK ON (AGAIN)

riot

conscience heavy helmets spark a riot
painting invisible battle lines
borders made of differentiating skin-colours
made uniform under a wash of blue
and
endless siren calls.

a statue toppled, swims,
escaping
in respite
then sinking into a black silty mud
cushioned by
shopping trolleys and ruined rusted bikes
for a pillow—made in China.

The shamed man's outline
lays silent, hoping for the melle to pass,
forgiveness that won't come,
soon to be dredged up, displayed
lasting moments set more in stone
with those marks
on an empty plinth
scratched with more resonance, relevance, than the form
it
once displayed.

forever scarred
fractured disowned moments of history
sunken pasts

always tainting the waterway's surfaces
felt forever, in the ebbs and flows of an ever-changing
city
—that will always be the same.

a tired population
generations marred, casualties of time
held in multi-torn arms
shaking with the ever-increasing weight
spectrum-filled tears co-join in a weeping city—
unable to forget
brought together in pain—anger
again and again
forced to repeat
unable to move on.

anchored by a not-so-distant history
misnamed shameful markers making sure
those cuts won't heal.

and—

echoes of hurt ripple in contradictions of waterways as
they swallow sunlight,
hope,
carrying peacocking sailboats.
as tourists walk the harbours
paths and banks
cut and cutting
with our souls bartering vessels of yesterday.

road rage

barely in sight,
another junction away,
as a stone chiselled jaw snaps at them, shouting.
yells filled with bloodiest hell.
a stubble—a burnt-black-smoking-forest,
their wandering non-committal indications,
slow driving,
make veins on his thick neck pulse harder and harder.
his fists grip a cracked black steering wheel
harder, harder.
tendons burn.
blood threatens to burst and trickle from hairy ears.

bang—a fist on the dash.

next, a life-worn tired old lady who's in a hurry too.
at her own pace,
trying to move her hips and knees,
which are taunted; stabbed by the needles inside.
she hobbles on...barely staying upright.
the crossing isn't the much-needed conveyor.
she wants to get her giro cashed,
get milk...some honey...biscuits for Fred.

the rage flows—out the windscreen at her.
stabbing.
the frail wounded old bird would be destroyed if she
turned...
saw, glimpsed his fury.

grips tighten, teeth grind—how dare she hold up his
progress,
to
nowhere.

now a van.
he yells.
an ambulance.
purest hate—'let them rot'.
now the police: don't get him started—he turns purple
with pent-up frustrations, buried sensitivities—emotions
free-flowing, expressed, blood-let.
from within a safe shield:
the iron womb of his car.

the moon slides slowly from behind leafy witnesses,
country lanes steer the wheels.
race him on.
veins carrying lead weights of hate and fury.

a small shape emerges on the horizon
moving hesitantly on the road...
wheels screech, as brakes bite.
with a foot stamp as if killing the last of his enemies.
his neck beats hard, then fades.
the stillness of the moonlight dances with the
streams of reaching headlights.

the window is rolled.
'go on son, off you go.'
a fist relaxes, reaching from a window—a finger wags,
gesturing to the roadside bushes.
saving the small quivering creature from sure death on
the road.
the creature slowly hops to safety, saved by a driver—

doomed to suffer with the bitter impatience
of his own slow death and relentless frictions with
humanity.

but, not with baby rabbits.

ships in the night

if my eyes caught yours
at the station
desiring a stranger's touch
to kill
more than time
—would you spare me 15 mins?
we could find a corner, a cubical
our own private cell.

if...we did,

would we miss our call?
forget our routes.
get lost in those scents
of new flesh.
—a wealth of pleasures.
beyond trivial trains to catch
and our dead-end destinations.
those tracks, maybe,
we were never meant to be on
anyway.

or...

would you cut me?
teach me not to leer at strangers
on a platform.
and, I'd be left grinning
on a slab,

as the coroner
struggles to break
the last smile from my face.

First published in Punk Noir Magazine

splinter foot

he never stops the jokes coming,
or those smiles.
with eyes that sparkle like stars.

with friends,
and alone, with the ghosts.
despite shell shock impairing
sounds of their laughter.
and
the afterglows of wars' flames,
shining harder than the smiles.

he rocks on,
back and forth—in that chair.
that never stops.

momentum to nowhere,
but the joy in living.
mind strewn in the Atlantic,
The North,
Indian.
seas and oceans that caught his friends.
drowned, burned, eaten up by fiery waters
—monsters of war.

still, he rocks on.
back and forth.
never stops with those jokes.

Harold could have been there,
but then it would have been *him*,
taken.
chewed up in foreign angry waters.

he laughs, jokes and smiles,
for those that can't—like Harold.
spreading warmth.
until he can't—
and only the memories of him remain.

radiating still after he's departed—in others he's
touched.
how he made them smile and laugh.
then was gone...
conjoined in loss with
those that rocked before him.

Sunday club massacre (at the Spotted Cow)

true worship lies in the grains of wood,
damp logoed mats,
and that dissonant hungover service.
by
staff addled,
pained
with the same cure, they dare dish out,
like the poisons served a night before.

one's church:
is an unstable seat in the corner,
over tacky floors.
where everyone talks,
no one listens.
where music blares during the day,
chosen earlier in the night.
by strangers,
before any sentiment mattered.

smells of food and drink linger,
tainted by those of bodies.
still, we desire, thirst for both.
in unhealthy measures.

money is taken,
never seen again,
transformed into waste products.
deposited, banked.

in backed-up drains, sewers reeking
with tales of disharmony,
fighting, blood.

in that, there's a love...

the power and the glory of it all,
Amen.

tainted portraits

beware smilers on-screen,
in shots
in an insta'.
they've knives out,
concealed behind doors,
in grey sorry
hate-stacked bedsits.

their neediness to show
a putty-filled shine
is dull
to everyone but them:
selling hard.
when,
they don't even buy it—
themselves.

by a book
think, listen.
stop the sad
race to faux fame.

things that truly shine,
are soon picked up by
the magpies of love,
radiators of joy,
on a plane to nowhere.

defy—

the relentless
screen-time pleading acceptance,
as they delay take-off.

take a breath, you'll live longer

he bounces off the walls, frantic—
buzzing about like a damn blue bottle.
boils a kettle, as if wrestling a tiger.
and, answers the phone, battling the cable
like it's a snake.
the world is against him in every way
and everything in it's a curse.
inanimate objects are his enemies,
whilst real enemies turn into ferocious demons.

he drives with everyone else on the road, the road itself,
signs and warnings, all an inconvenience to his route—
this path he's chosen, also a wild goose chase and a
foolish errand.

nothing makes sense,
because he doesn't stop long enough
pause,
take that breath.
food is fuel
and he can't get it in quick enough.
when it hits the pit of his stomach
his metabolism is shocked,
then comes the pause
slowing
time to reflect
nap even,
before the next tiger comes calling
and the buzzing starts over

next time with a full belly
and a smile.

the line is dead

my hand sticks to a payphone receiver,
covered in scratches, words by idle hands,
ritualistically reporting in.
as they call home.
because that's what you do.
when expected to be found hanging onto apron strings,
from a distance, past tower blocks,
motorways,
music.
endless brick walls of rain.
in the stark reality,
darkness of an empty room.

finally pushed out, to look past the dinner table,
and the fence at the bottom of the garden.

'hello.'
'yes.'
'you okay?'
'yes.'
'met any friends yet?'
'yes,' a lie.
'met a girl yet?'
'yes.'
'as long as she's one of us.'
'yes, she is,' a lie.
'well, speak soon…'
'yes.'
'glad you're okay, enjoying yourself, safe.'

outside, sirens scream.
rain washes blood off roads.
a sword is wiped.
a stranger's body falls over—headless.
people watch, walk on.
others look on from my block.

I am okay.
But, safe?
I might go outside, to see if I am in fact
enjoying it.
and if I can watch the bodies pile up, headless, like the
others.
watch the blood pooling, as if it's all normal.
just like back then, sitting at the end of that kitchen table,
or,
like another knot in that old garden fence
as it waited to be pushed through for me to see what was
on the other side.

tooth fairy

I remember shards, sharp little edges,
hollow innards and jagged sides.
I'd nudge, tease and push with an eager tongue:
toying, working away—
at those stubborn little baby pegs.

at the dinner table, I'd try to do it secretly;
wobble discreetly,
tweak with my tongue,
for fear of the ex-territorial army angry man threatening
to get his pliers,
or tie it to a door knob,
again.

he soon left—
pub…

eventually, with a last taut bit of skin hanging on
and pulled by my impatient hand, it would
snap
free
with a taste of
iron and a
pop
of relief.
for now,
from the pliers
the door swing
…from the beer-soaked angry breath.

this angry man would always be out by then, standing at
a warm bar,
at night, alone.
he couldn't afford to drink until he couldn't stand
anymore...but he did.

back home,
as each tooth fell, I'd have an extra blanket to stay warm,
and a cat on my pillow.
mum could never afford the 50p for the electricity meter;
pissed away on beer fueled
ex-territorial streams against walls and lamp posts.

despite this:
cold, cats on pillows and
ice on the inside—

in the morning, as condensation melted and rolled down
my window,
the tooth fairy
had always
left a 50p coin
under my pillow

that I'd give to mum.

vanishing point

responsibilities burn
on life-draining commutes.
destinations, once unwritten.
now begging for the pen on loan
and paper,
borrowed too.
as the man slowly rots,
professionally married
to—
a soulless dog-machine.

the company car air
grows thicker by the minute,
a rolled window adds
fumes to the wake.

he mourns freedoms lost,
swallowed under tyres of the cars in front.
his mind is blank and pulse dead
before wrestling to park.

on fairer days,
the four wheels are swapped for two.
in hopes of a glowing daydream:
that someday...
the horizon
will become that constantly moving target.
open legs, drawing him in.
that he'll grin, chasing.

the joy of freedom in moving,
never reaching a final destination.

walking towards the noise

against the rusted gates of Heaven is a weary face of a
woman,
tested by time,
made more testing by men.
she looks through,
uncertain if she wants past.

when it all stops,
everything done,
God finally sees her,
just as she is turning away,
despaired.

God is left, questioning the side (s)he's on.
outside looking in,
made weary too
by the experiment: failed.

will she turn back, to face the creator?
or, take the hand of her lover,
never turning,
looking ahead.
and walk calmly towards the noise.

Thank You

About the Author

John Bowie was born in Northumberland, Northern England and studied in Manchester in the '90s. He has published poetry, novels and short stories. He now lives in Bristol, U.K.

John is the founder and editor-in-chief of Bristol Noir.

If you can spare a few minutes…

Please leave a review on Goodreads and Amazon.

WWW.BRISTOLNOIR.CO.UK

© BRISTOL NOIR, 2022

Also out now

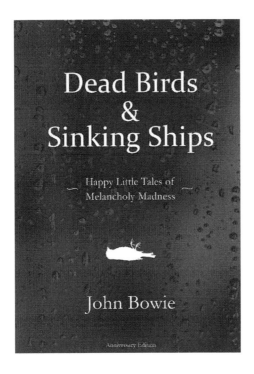

'Bowie's poetry is brutal and lyrical, beautifully textured, almost palpable. In Dead Birds & Sinking Ships, he depicts the contradictory world in which he grew up. A world of nature against urbanisation, reason against madness, a world of fights, real and imaginary, a world in which love, war, loneliness and trauma cohabit, that he exposes it in all its fascinating cruelty. A wonderful collection...'

— B F Jones, author of Something Happened at 2 a.m.

Also out now

BLACK VIKING THRILLER #1

John Bowie

UNTETHEЯED
[DREAMS OF FUTURE MEMORIES]

'*Set in 1998 in Bristol, England, Bowie's dark, hard-edged crime novel Untethered inaugurates a promising series.*'

— **Publishers Weekly**

'*Noir fans will find a lot to like.*'

— **BookLife**

Printed in Great Britain
by Amazon

27294280R00053